Don't misplace the moon

Don't misplace the moon

Poems by

Annie Stenzel

© 2024 Annie Stenzel. All rights reserved.
This material may not be reproduced in any form, published,
reprinted, recorded, performed, broadcast,
rewritten or redistributed without
the explicit permission of Annie Stenzel.
All such actions are strictly prohibited by law.

Cover design by Shay Culligan
Cover image by Alexis Rhone Fancher
Author photo by Rick Ross

ISBN: 978-1-63980-585-3

Kelsay Books
502 South 1040 East, A-119
American Fork, Utah 84003
Kelsaybooks.com

for my family, larger than it looks

The Gratitudes

Now that I have studied the front matter of many other poets' collections, I see that "there are too many people to name" is a common lament for any writer fortunate enough to publish a collection of poetry. It is a strange world out there, and for many of us the process of getting a book into readers' hands is a very long haul. So I am grateful for encouragements of various kinds that kept me from throwing my hands up in despair during the years it took from the first iteration of this manuscript to evolve into the version you are reading. Even being told "this came close" could bolster my conviction that perseverance was desirable, and the fact that the collection, under a different title, was a finalist early on for the Washington Prize at The Word Works did a lot to sustain my belief that there was merit in the work. Finding homes for many of the individual poems in publications, both online and in print, also kept the spark of determination alight. And landing the manuscript in the amazing hands of Kelsay Books was the fulfilment of my long hope for this collection. Thank you, Karen Kelsay and the rest of the team.

I have for a number of years participated with a group of writers in what I might call "the prod project." The idea is that we e-mail the draft of a piece of writing to the other members once a week. Some participate faithfully; others only rarely. There is no requirement that we respond to one another's drafts. Some offer detailed critiques, and others never say a word. But taking part in the prod project has been of considerable use to me, and it was indispensable to me during the worst of the pandemic. Plentiful thanks are therefore due to Melanie Perish, Nancy Harris McLelland, Judith Rodby, Katherine Case, Vivian Olds, Sonne B., and Patricia Caspers for helping me keep the writing wheels rolling.

In 2019, I began attending a retreat that was held at a former convent in San Rafael, California. Writers and visual artists congregated for two or three days in an extraordinary setting, and being at Santa Sabina was a boon for anyone with even a tiny creative bone in her body: a number of the poems in this collection were begun or worked on there. To Susan Ito, then, the incredible force behind this annual event, and to the dozens of women I shared space and time with there, abundant thanks for the pleasure of your company, plenty of prompts, and the shared space for turning words into poems. (This is where the "too many to name" really kicks in; but I'm sure that my Santa Sabina companions know who they are.)

After the retreat that took place in 2020, a couple of us who live in the Bay Area began to get together in coffee shops from time to time to channel the energy of Santa Sabina. And then along came the lockdown . . . and like everyone else we immediately shifted gears to the Zoom environment and reconstituted ourselves as "writers at the crack of dawn." Twice a week, first thing in the morning, at home in our nightclothes, the three of us met virtually, and kept each other company as we pursued whatever creative thread unfolded in front of us. To Heather Bourbeau and especially to Lisa Hsia, heartfelt appreciation for keeping me company and helping me return, again and again, to the task of shaping what I want to say into a poem, or what William Carlos Williams wonderfully described as "a small (or large) machine made of words."

Under the heading of "excellent friends I have never met face to face" is a contingent I know only through that strange phenomenon, social media: a gathering of women and non-binary writers who populate a very active and encouraging Facebook group. I have had support for my work from these people that has buoyed me immeasurably over the years, so here's looking at you, Binders; thanks for being there.

Asking fellow poets to write a blurb for my book required a deep breath and overcoming a lot of trepidation. To Francesca Bell, Jessica Goodfellow, and Romana Iorga for their generosity in taking the time to read the manuscript, and then to write things about my work that I can only hope the collection lives up to, I offer bountiful gratitude.

I have three living siblings, and they support my passion for poetry with plenty of encouragement. To Julius, Kate, and John, thank you for having my back, even though complications of geography prevent us from spending anywhere near as much time together as we would like. I love you to bits and pieces, as we say. And I have a group of cousin-ish family members who have brought great joy into my life in the years since we connected; you all have a place here too.

There was no doubt in my mind whose photography I wanted for the cover of this book: many thanks to Alexis Rhone Fancher for allowing me to use one of her amazing images. And I'm squeamish about seeing pictures of myself, so I was very lucky Rick Ross made the author photo process quite painless.

Once upon a time, I would have rolled my eyes at the idea that a grown-up could possibly boast about having a *bestie*. For my poetry life, however, I am lucky enough to have one. She and I conjure mini-retreats to a variety of beautiful locations where we sip tasty lattes in coffee shops and revel in having permission to focus exclusively on our writing. We are endlessly fascinated by the subject of poetry, and embrace the goal of making the poems we write as cogent and as potent as possible. This book would never have made it to print without you, Patricia Caspers.

Lastly, I am indebted to Audre Lorde, Bruce Lee, Eduardo C. Corral, Antonio Machado, Dylan Thomas, Elizabeth Bishop, André Breton, and René Magritte for phrases or lines from their work that were the portal into my writing a handful of these poems.

Acknowledgements

A number of the poems in this manuscript have been published, some with different titles or in slightly different forms. Grateful acknowledgement is made to the journals in which those poems originally appeared.

Amaryllis: "Dictionary II"
Anti-heroin chic: "Object permanence"
Atlanta Review: "House moving 'rained out'"
Atlas and Alice: "Come, cup of tea, and bid me write morning"
The Bitchin' Kitsch: "Why did I do that solitary deed?"
Chestnut Review: "On learning of the death by suicide of an 11-year-old boy I didn't know"
Door is a jar: "When summer conjures winter in the mind"
Eclectica: "Two messengers speak, in passing," "Spectrum"
The Ekphrastic Review: "Still scraping the floor"
FERAL A journal of poetry and art: "A question"
Gargoyle: "How to tame a tarantula"
Gone Lawn: "palimpsest"
Halfway down the stairs: "Consider two comrades, quiet and silence"
isacoustic: "(This is the alternative)"
Kestrel: "Countdown"
K'in Literary Journal: "After I dream about geophagia"
The Lake: "Greed," "Moratorium"
Lily Poetry Review: "Blumenfenster"
Negative Capability Press: "Before we all took names"
Night Heron Barks: "Meditation on mortality with a line from a poem by Antonio Machado embedded in it"
Nixes Mate: "Cronos devoured his children," "Misreading leads me to sundry wonders"
On the Seawall: "The Auspices"

One Art Poetry: "Incarnation," "Let the skull be a bowl," "The dreamery"
Pine Hills Review: "Nightmared"
Poets Reading the News: "All by ourselves, regardless"
Psaltery & Lyre: "In the forest, birdsong echoes"
The Ravens Perch: "Portent," "Everything we see hides another thing," "Is it true?"
Redheaded Stepchild: "An apple is its own whole poem"
Riddled with Arrows: "To this day, we do not know the range of their vocabulary"
right hand pointing: "Nine lines of just nine syllables each," "To the lilies in a strange-shaped vase"
Rust & Moth: "Shelter. Cage"
Saranac Review: "A ghazal is always within reach of pain"
Shot Glass Journal: "Dust, and yet, not dust"
Slipstream: "Shall I call you mother's milk or mother's ruin?"
South Florida Poetry Journal: "Loneliness arrives on a leash of scorpions"
Stirring: "Carried, or buoyed"
Streetlight Magazine: "Reliquary"
SWWIM: "Summoned"
Thimble Lit Mag: "Scarlet gerbera," "Lately, certain months decline their customary duty"
Third Wednesday: "Dwindle"
Trampoline Poetry: "Hobson's Choice"
UCity Review: "Maybe I was eight years old. Maybe nine"
Uppagus: "The word 'cauterize' has fallen out of favor," "After the move, there are new things to write 100 times on a piece of paper"
Writing in a Woman's Voice: "Forbidden," "Skin hunger"

Contents

To the lilies in a strange-shaped vase   19

One

Misreading leads me to sundry wonders   23
Cronos devoured his children   24
Dictionary II   25
Summoned   26
Shelter. Cage.   27
An apple is its own whole poem   28
How to tame a tarantula   29
Scarlet gerbera   30
In the forest, birdsong echoes   31
Come, cup of tea, and bid me write morning   32
After the move, there are new things to write
    100 times on a sheet of paper   33

Two

To this day, we do not know the range of their
    vocabulary   37
Hobson's Choice   38
After I dream about geophagia   39
A question   40
Is it true?   41
Dust, and yet, not dust   42
Nine lines of just nine syllables each   43
All by ourselves, regardless   44
(This is the alternative)   45
"Loneliness arrives on a leash of scorpions."   46

Three

Meditation on mortality with a line from a poem by Antonio Machado embedded in it	49
Shall I call you mother's milk or mother's ruin?	50
When summer conjures winter in the mind	51
palimpsest	52
Ode to plainfin midshipman	53
Object permanence	55
Why did I do that solitary deed?	56
The word "cauterize" has fallen out of favor	57
On learning of the death by suicide of an 11-year-old boy I didn't know	58
A ghazal is always within reach of pain	59
Greed	61
Forbidden	62
Reliquary	63
Before we all took names	64

Four

Let the skull be a bowl	67
Still Scraping the Floor	68
Maybe I was eight years old. Maybe nine.	69
"Blumenfenster"	70
The dreamery	71
"House moving 'rained-out'"	72
The Auspices	73
Nightmared	74
Dwindle	75
Spectrum	76

Two messengers speak, in passing	77
Countdown	78
Incarnation	79
"Skin hunger"	80
Moratorium	81
Lately, certain months decline their customary duty	82
Consider two comrades, quiet and silence	83
"Everything we see hides another thing"	84
Carried, or buoyed	85

To the lilies in a strange-shaped vase

I think I'll let you go today
before your beauty
changes to decay and your petals
into ghosts of their quick glory.

Some people are opposed to flowers
cut and sold, doomed to languish
indoors for a fraction of the lives they'd lead
connected to the ground or tree.

Forgive me. There are times I need
to be force-fed this lesson in mortality.
Say what you will, these lilies
had a job to do, and did it well.

One

Misreading leads me to sundry wonders

Like the time I read the Audre Lorde line

love is a word another kind of open

just a little wrong
and thought it said

love is a new kind of apron

which in one sense I guess it can be:
a robust amour-propre can help
keep the world's worst soil

off my fancy outfit. After all
these years solo, I am not the object
of anyone else's ardor—I must lap

myself with suitable expressions
of affection to avoid
the cold stain of indifference.

Which is not always
an easy job. Once bloom and beauty
wane, the knee-jerk of *ooh-love*

and *ah-love* from other quarters
subsides. But the original pump
for this essence may simply

want priming. Get to work
beneath the apron. A half-teaspoon
of self-love siphoned into your pocket

may turn out to be
plenty.

Cronos devoured his children

If only there were merely space between us
and not that bastard, Time, bulging at the seams

with his accumulated potency. Distance
is one thing. Those of us who are able still

scissor several miles into manageable strides each day
leaving the warm air to close behind us, our footsteps

safely tucked into the space between Points A
and B. Begin, proceed, arrive. Repeat.

All that takes place in the barefaced moment
called Now. But what if the journey to be undertaken

stumbles at the border, where the abyss always
yawns, where the guardian of that fatal gap

won't hear a plea for mercy or forgiveness?
You show me an hourglass. The sand never moves.

Dictionary II

More often found these days
in an old library than
an everyday living-room,
outsized volumes
slump in silence

each tome
a fully-furnished palace—
room upon room filled
with words
rarely spoken aloud

languages in casual
or deliberate contact;
brushing against one another
here delicately
there bluntly.

Now silverfish slide
between the pages
where words
are stacked in silent columns:
clambake to *clarity*

roulade to *Rousseau,*
wharf to *wheel.*

Summoned

(with a deep bow to Bruce Lee)

That's when she said it: *be like water.*
or maybe it was, *Oh Annie!*
just be like water.
And I wanted to, then.

But water behaves or misbehaves
in all sorts of mysterious ways.

Ocean-water alone does a dozen
different things—before breakfast.

The Mississippi is a different creature
from the Nile.

And what about ice,
which is absolute water.

Or water forced by a massive dam
to drown a canyon? That's one thing.

The run-off after helicopters dump
scooped-up water on a wildfire? Another.

Or maybe she meant a forest pool, quietly
hosting water-striders.

Well, remember how shocked we were,
in science class, to find out
the human body is 60 percent H_2O?
I'm already a quick cascade through a weir.

Shelter. Cage.

Somebody made it elliptical, not angular:
Things that start one-where end
elsewhere. You keep trying, even if thwarted
when, on a grey day, the sun won't work
as a talisman. Might as well be in a maze.

Trumpetvine, wisteria, plus princess flower.
Bougainvillea, with its irksome papery tidbits
dusting the ground. Jasmine that startles you
when its musky hints appear. And what a bother:
the tiny pink rose is mostly eclipsed, too high to see.

What do you think you are doing here,
behind such a complex hedge? A gardener
deals with the tangle, but whose strange
idea was it to cluster these motley plantings
around the patio? And then allow a serpent of ivy in.

An apple is its own whole poem

Sometimes you get an apple so divine
it makes you believe you're Eve.

Sometimes when you hold the solid globe—
a Cameo or a Honeycrisp—
and cut neat slices with your knife
the fragrance makes you swoon.

Sometimes the shout of flavor
from that first bite arrests your
jaw, incredulous, before you
can chew and swallow the delight:
the juice and texture such a leap
of wisdom in your mouth

of course you want to share it
with the starving world.

How to tame a tarantula

First, a question: must you even try?
Wouldn't you rather
leave your tarantula right
where you found it,
hustling across the pot-holed road?

You could still call it "your" tarantula,
but it would belong to itself, picking
its own meals from crickets and voles,
choosing for itself when to take
the many hours it requires of repose.

Another question: are you willing to commit
to 20 years with your tarantula? The females
can live that long. But remember: she won't
do tricks, she isn't keen on being petted, and even
a small fall may be fatal. She's that fragile.

Before I tell you how to tame
a tarantula, I'll ask you one more time:
why bother? All those legs will always
want to run off without you. Plus
you're a daytime person. She loves the night.

Scarlet gerbera

No leaf, no fern for company
nothing but the bright of this red
stands up to a dim that would engulf me.

Moving stands third on a list
of life-stressors, right after a loved one's
death, and divorce.

Aren't I too old for this? I'm quite as averse
to displacement as I am to other tectonic
forces: only two addresses in 25 years.

So I plucked the cellophane-wrapped
bunch of daisies from a pail
at the supermarket, took them home

and placed them in the vase I hadn't
packed yet. All week they dazzled
the table before the first one bent

its head, petals drooping, almost as though
sending forth a sigh, if store-bought
flowers could.

In the forest, birdsong echoes

how can I, how can I
is not what the songbird said
but something similar

who were we, we who set out
on a day on a walk through the woods
to a new, a new, another new place

how is it we thought the forest
and the trees were part and parcel?
part of this, part of that, part of
why did you, why did you

in the forest, trees, and the trees
see only themselves and not the forest
or the birds

the eyes of most songbirds look to either
side, rather than forward
but the eyes of birds that have died look up

and see nothing in the forest

where birdsong still echoes

Come, cup of tea, and bid me write morning

Every day, a portal opens, only
to snap closed, catching part of me—
a camera's shutter, a piece of origami
folded with more passion than skill.

Every day, what of the words snipped
out of a mind teeming with words?
Ah, listen! how often language rings me
like a sympathetic bell.

Clasped hands, surely you remember
every touch from the bewilderment
of butterflies who chose as a landing place some
stretch of skin—your wrist, or cheek, or shin?

Dear hands that have never touched
a harp's strings; hands that would never wish
to wield a dagger—can you at least speak truth
using this nib that scritches on a naked page?

After the move, there are new things to write
100 times on a sheet of paper

I will mitigate chronic grumbles with occasional
        slices of watermelon
I will acquiesce to opportunities for sudden bliss
I will recite the names of friendly new neighbors,
        their pets included
I will quell the urge to hang wet sheets on a phantom clothesline
I will keep *Comfortable with Uncertainty* close to hand
I will simulate contentment until the real thing fits
        like a soft sweater
I will lift the needle from the turntable before it plays
        a dangerous song

        On the other side of the page, these:

I must not pave a new rut with old regret
I must not try to exit the wrong door
I must not turn savage when I cannot find my lost purpose
        in the other room
I must not heap coals of annoyance on dead embers
I must not mistake inconvenience for cataclysm
I must not disturb the new breed of sleeping dog
I must not misplace the moon

Two

To this day, we do not know the range of their vocabulary

When you live in the half-dark, your spirit seeks
a window; given clay, your hands shape vessels

or figures of your desire. So, on the cave wall, why not
place your inky hands to show the creatures all belong

to you—great beasts to feed the hunger of ten
families? Why not draw pictures, each one

more eloquent than the one before, more vivid
as your eyes increase their skill, your hands

learn how to capture accurately the animals' proportions;
until your final picture is worth a thousand words

and you did not need to use any of them.

Hobson's Choice

I used to say, *nobody got here first,* and all I meant by that
was, the forest primeval predates us humans. But little
did the long array of living creatures know they had no right
to their own environment. Silly me, thinking
of the rights of sycamore, the rights of moving waters,
a thorn bug's or an osprey's or an aardvark's
right to live according

to some particular weft and warp of nature. Never mind
how it all unfolded, stardust to prokaryote to great ape;
isn't it enough that there once was a time before needless
avarice? A tern robs a pelican; the Nile crocodile grabs
its meal from a hyena, which robbed it from a cheetah
which brought the impala down. Oh well.

How long ago did generosity arrive? Prosocial behavior
within a species likely came first, but
what happened next? How quickly did we get
to Romulus and Remus, raised by wolves, fed
by woodpecker? We'll never know the name of the very
first swimmer saved by dolphins, or the elephant

who would not drop the log it carried into the trench
where a dog was sleeping despite the mahout's urging.
So, over the millennia, perhaps those who flourished
were the ones who shared? Perhaps *do unto others, including
the moth and the mountain tarn* worked well for our
foreparents. Until it all got muddled.

An old cartoon you've surely seen, fish in sizes
descending from large to small across the single panel,
each fish with its mouth agape except for one
who looks over its shoulder at the following flounder
with an expression of dismay. Eat or be eaten.
Or eat, and then be eaten.

After I dream about geophagia

Yes, I keep a few green things alive—indoors—and I'm
the one my neighbors ask to water their tomatoes, roses,
herbs. Nothing dies on my watch, though I would be a liar

if I said all of my charges thrive. A rubber plant
on its last legs, gasps in a clay pot outdoors. I can't
seem to put it out of its misery. Of course it was a gift

when I moved here years ago, and for a while
it stretched sturdy leaves up toward the ceiling.
When it grew too tall for its table-space I severed

a hefty chunk of trunk and leaves to keep it domesticated,
but then I guess my little place turned hostile. Hence,
exile to the porch, close to the compost.

Some people yearn for this: to lift a handful
of soil, worms or no worms, to hold it up to the curious
mouth, to take a taste of the earth's beloved surface.

On certain mornings, early and alone, I step outside
onto the yielding ground, study the garden, know
hunger, and imagine.

A question

Why don't we ever say *sky me*

the way we say *tree me*
when I, a hapless creature, am being pursued;

the way we say *water me*
when all I emit is rasps, I am so parched;

and the way we say *ground me*
when electrical surges put me at risk;

or the way we say *air me*
when, after too many months enclosed, I venture out of doors?

Language finds itself at a loss when a new situation
wants words to scaffold it.

But how can I tell you what I mean by *sky me*
when it hasn't happened yet, and may never?

Is it true?

that someone could walk this mountain road and know
the name of every single tree that stands along the way?
If so, who are you, and do these lovelies speak in leafy
tongues, telling you soil and water tales, stories
of too much sun, the absence of bees, how much it pains
them (if it does!) to feel the stab of woodpecker beaks?

Do the trees say how glad they are to hear the first peeps
from the chicks that hatch from eggs of the great horned
owl? And, when firestorms leave trees lifeless
but still standing as charred poles, do the tree-ghosts
sigh with you as you wonder: who will be alive years hence
when new trees, staunch and green, line the road?

Dust, and yet, not dust

(after a photo of Colette, "Reve d'Egypte")

All month, I watched one woman's face, caught her glance
because her eyes followed me around this small room. Grainy
in black-and-white, the image is so dated there can be no doubt:
a camera clicked and caught this shot a long lifetime ago.

Even not knowing whose it was, I was still convinced
that face would age but perhaps didn't if the subject died young.
Those haunted eyes developed cataracts or maybe
none, before they closed one final time.
Never again could the sloe eyes send a message to the mind

inside the skull hidden beneath the tousled curls. Yet,
here she is still, staring at me the way she peered
from the calendar in March last year,
and just the way she mesmerized a photographer in 1907.
A picture is protection from death's erasure of a single day.

What more do you need, Colette? The life you led,
the words you left, and now this other kind of immortality.

Nine lines of just nine syllables each

Nothing to be done. I say again:
Do nothing. Now face due west. Repeat.
The rose of the winds will not help you.

To use another's voice is pointless.
You'll be mute on a ship in a storm.
Box the compass. Choose the obscure way.

Pretend you were once a pirate queen.
That island where you buried treasure—
marked on a map you drew in the sand.

All by ourselves, regardless

me and all my wants, you and your wants, we sit
on the same side of the same table.

me and my wants, many of which are unreasonable,
some of which are mutually exclusive;

you and your wants . . . say what you will
about them, as I only know what you tell me

though I hear enough to believe you merely
want whatever you want, regardless.

elsewhere on the globe, other yous, their
wants also strident, distinct from ours.

we and all our wants, side by side, our elbows
on the table, a table now massively extended

to accommodate so many wants, the table called
upon to accommodate more more more—

one table, thrown forth by the planet's
last, lovely, irreplaceable heartwood

and the table would have plenty to say
but it is mute, even as it trembles.

(This is the alternative)

On a day when almost everything is too much effort
it turns out I am holding a banana in one hand
and not for the first time, either:
hardly anything enjoys the privilege of uniqueness.

It turned out I was holding a banana in one hand
while I stared out the dirty window to the street.
Hardly anything suffers the stigma of uniqueness.
There is a reason: we would be frightened, and we already are.

While I was staring out the window to the street
I was also trying to keep certain thoughts at bay
and for good reason: I can be frightened, and I am.
As it was, I tried to hear the freeway sounds as soothing.

There I lay, trying to keep thoughts at bay
but they were like fish that jump into the boat while you're rowing!
I tried hard to hear the freeway noise as soothing
and not as the sound of tumbrels, advancing on the Place de Grève.

I'm serious: once a fish did jump into an eight I was rowing.
You wouldn't read about it! the doctor at 5-seat exclaimed
but he'd never heard tumbrels, advancing on the Place de Grève.
Enough about Paris . . . that was then; this is now.

That fellow at 5-seat never read about it, silly doctor.
Many people are squeamish about flights of the imagination.
But enough about Paris: that was then; this is surely now.
And remember that most old lakes are difficult to navigate.

Aren't we all somewhat squeamish? Imagination takes flight
and not for the last time, either:
They say old lakes are the most difficult to navigate
on a day when everything is almost too much effort.

"Loneliness arrives on a leash of scorpions."

But my dream world is filled with people, colorful and kind
plus people you haven't met if you don't read Austen or Dumas.
Shake hands, please, with people now dead. Feel free to shiver.
Now meet some of the people I whittled from blocks of soft wood.

My mother knitted characters from books. And painted people?
Grey people mingle with the pink, as in old and young.
People I have only imagined, conjuring them in two dimensions.
Most people are eclipsed from time to time. Or cloud-hidden.

Certain people are regularly gauzed with the stain of morning light
but only if they hunger for beauty. Other people are cloaked
in mystery, aghast when they collide with people fully visible.
It is clear no one will tell me, *your people shall be my people.*

And no one can argue with this claim: People *are* strange.
Which means lonely people are everywhere, always.
And that's just another E-minor earworm.

The title of this poem appears in Eduardo C. Corral's poem, "Lines Written During My Second Pandemic," which was published online as the Poem-a-Day for October 31, 2022 by the Academy of American Poets.

Three

Meditation on mortality with a line from a poem by Antonio Machado embedded in it

When you are young, there is no such thing
as death, other than the death of days, celebrated
by scarlet sunsets, or the death of leaves, deliberately
put before you in Technicolor. Oh yes—ants succumb

during picnics, flies must be swatted, and the little turtle
that trudged in circles around its plastic domain
and seemed to sleep beneath the phony palm tree. One day
it will be there, not all that interesting. The next, gone.

But at a given moment, the scenery will change, as though
behind the curtain during a pause at the opera.
The great-aunt you hardly knew will be described
as having *died*. It turns out, traveler, there is no road;

the road is made by walking. And you may believe
you get to choose where you are headed. You do not.

The line, "traveler, there is no road; the road is made by walking" appears in Antonio Machado's *Proverbs and Songs, #29*

Shall I call you mother's milk or mother's ruin?

Here comes my dead mother, clutching a square
bottle and only a little unsteady on her pins.

I could have earned a merit badge in Martinis
in my Girl Scout days. The formula she taught

stuck with me . . . three jiggers of gin; scant half jigger
of vermouth; noisy cubes of ice dropped into a glass vessel

and just like 007's concoction, always shaken, never stirred.
An olive—stuffed, by preference—or in a pinch

with its irksome pit. The chilly glass delivered to my mother
as she utters this injunction: *spill not one drop!*

Later, she forswore fidelity to the frosted
bottle. And why? I guess Gilbey's got too pricey.

Then my services as bartender ceased to be required
and the cheapest gin, served in a plastic tumbler (don't bother

with the waft of vermouth) became the order of the day.
Of every long day, to the end of her days, with words that slurred

and the smoldering stubs of Raleigh plain-ends
reeking in the ashtray. Her cough was another story.

> Today, just down the block, the gardener
> chopped a juniper that overflowed
>
> the devil strip, releasing the power of bruised berries
> into the air: scent of gin, ghost message from my mother.

When summer conjures winter in the mind

then carve me a place to stand on the mountain
and let the gusts press cold against me

arbitrarily. A caprice of clouds overhead
will change the light, shadow to blaze.

There I will witness the struggle of trees wedged
between granite and sky; how little soil

clings in a setting careless
for the requirements of what survives.

Sometimes, the blessing is strict: simply *not*
to have the means of self-destruction.

The mercy is one hand without a dagger,
the other empty of poison or gun.

palimpsest

after the scare
a scar forms

      the scar
      reminds you of the scare

           a new scare?
           another scar

      fast forward
      for the score:

if the scare is mere
you survive

           chances are, the final scare
           you won't remember

Ode to plainfin midshipman

At first, revulsion blinded me. I used my own harsh labels
and condemned *Porichthys notatus*—a toadfish.

But now that I know more, I've carefully removed *ew!*
and *ugly,* from my response to this interesting
creature, whose reproductive style alone was a big surprise.

The music was another. For years we've known that humpback
whales could sing, and dolphins' clicks and whistles signal
various significant things. But when I conjure water dwellers,

their voices are rarely part of the package. And yet in Sausalito,
some years back, a whole marina of houseboat residents
was puzzled every summer night by a noise no one

could figure out. And everyone marveled when an answer
to the mystery arrived at last: in breeding season
male toadfish hum. Whoa. Then females are summoned

to whichever sound best seduces, and they lay their eggs.
But it was the video I saw, with the scientist carefully
lifting a rock at low tide, that altered my attitude once and for all:

Flurried by the unexpected exposure—with hundreds of eggs
close-quartered on the bottom of the rock—a male
plainfin midshipman dashed and splashed across his small domain,

desperate to avoid the intruder's hands. For he's the one
who'll occupy a dark, protected nursery until the eggs
have hatched. Which takes a month, and then he tends

the toadlets for a few more weeks until they leave the nest.
Who knew? In the marina, those houseboat residents
were still not happy about the fishes' nightly noise, but

summer only lasts a few quick months, and then
plainfin midshipmen return to the deep where,
more than a hundred fathoms down, their photophores draw

food to them through autumn, winter, and spring, when
intertidal waters draw them back and it's time for the fish
to start singing again.

Object permanence

The flight of youth a bit like a moon rocket
Infant to ancient. Innocence to experience
Barely a trace of tender left by the time childhood is complete
Seems like the word *heedless* says it all
But at the helm, is anyone paying attention?
You'd think grabbing an old photograph might be useful
In my case, very small images in black and white
I was pale, the pictures were blurred, my hair was curly—

I was pale, the pictures were blurred, my hair was curly—
In my case, very small images in black and white
You'd think grabbing an old photograph might be useful
But at the helm, is anyone paying attention?
Seems like the word *heedless* says it all
Barely a trace of tender left by the time childhood is complete
Infant to ancient. Innocence to experience
The flight of youth a bit like a moon rocket

Why did I do that solitary deed?

(for, and after, Dylan Thomas)

Because I had to help myself
that spring.
Because I witnessed the silky way
white petals caught in wind-drifts
floated through the forest dust-motes
and in warm light
mingled with the sound
of fervent birds, among them
a hermit thrush, I think it was.
Or Swainson's, maybe.

And I was all alone, a righteous
miracle in those crowded days—I had distanced
myself from the cluster of tent cabins,
marched my sturdy boots a mile away
from my kind, only to find
my body urgent
for another species of escape.

I told myself: *this is a Thing
you never!* and surely didn't think I'd ever
dare to do outdoors, with the sky watching.
But after all was whispered and complete
it was the same force moved me—the one
that through the green fuse drives the flower.

That's why I did the deed
alone in the mountains, my back
against the bark of a warm tree,
my shirt and shorts in disarray,
my breath more and more ragged,
and my hands: two dear friends
touching me.

The word "cauterize" has fallen out of favor

Most sources claim, to treat
a wound by searing flesh
had its heyday in the middle
of the 19th Century.

In several countries, blood-soaked
battlefields meant mostly doom
for those who were merely injured.
Red-hot blades might save a soldier

from the loss of a limb. Or not.
But is it wise to cauterize
a before-wound?
Even if the site is known,

perhaps even the width
and depth to which the gash
will penetrate beneath
a spongy surface?

Be warned: dread
is its own harbinger.
Don't be too quick
to brandish flaming sword

above your flesh—the skin
intact but wary, ready
to cringe from an insult that is still
several days distant.

On learning of the death by suicide of an 11-year-old boy I didn't know

My first response is incredulity: eyes wide
in hope of having misread the message. Moisture
scratch-leaps to make tears; throat catches because
breath won't pass through paralysis. Pity
and sympathy hand in hand with horror.

By the time compassion comes, I can't
un-know how altered that poor family's
life will be, split into before and after, never
resuming its former course, each year the landmark
anniversary with its mountain of wrecked hopes.

Into the echoes that separate me from true grief,
my hands lift to wring and plead. I want to shriek
at the phantom youth: Oh, child! you have murdered
the wrong person. The boy you killed was only
a stranger passing through whoever you were going to be.

A ghazal is always within reach of pain

Evidence in one spot on the right ankle. Ancient souvenir of trip,
    fall, gash, then heal
but leaving three scars that linger decades after the ragged wounds
    all healed.

Two hardworking parents, five children, hundreds of raucous,
    squabbling meals.
Loaf after loaf of bread your mother baked. Luckily, you were
    content with the heel.

At this stage of the messy proceedings known as a life, scars and
    afflictions accrue
in impressive numbers. When the asteroid strikes, there's a crater
    that won't heal.

You limp along a trail that angles up and down, fraught with limbs
    and roots.
Do you hike in tall boots? And they fit, but five miles in, here's
    a blister on your heel.

Oh no, says the heart! A pang, a twinge of memory quick to
    overwhelm with tears
that say sorrow, leak grief, wail woe. Trigger endless, unsuccessful
    efforts to heal.

The news from a much-loved cousin stops you cold, quick salt
    geysering: It's cancer.
Rare. Fast-growing. Two major organs affected, and a lymph node,
    too. He'll

know more in a few days, crisscrossing the city to see an array of
	experts, but
even they can't say more than *few recover from this mixture.
	Some heal*

*and return to their lives, their hikes, their many loves, a family and
	its sweet histories.*
Others don't. Too many won't. Being alive is a wound that won't
	heal.

Greed

Through a moment's grace I am allowed to see
a streak of starlight hasten past the window—
shallow arc inscribed briefly on the indigo.

Instantly my heart demands: another
shooting star to send it soaring. And if my wish
were granted, I would want, again, another.

The hard-edged prism of desire is a tricky thing
when the walls close in. Can you tell me, sans
perjury, you have ever passed an hour without

the words *I want* trembling in your mouth?

Forbidden

The neighbor's sign is unequivocal: *don't even think
about these apples on my tree.* But he can't stop me.

>I stare at those orbs and let my thoughts
>water, my mouth go wild.

>Was an apple my first fruit? Who can say.
>No one is left to quiz on the subject.

Another neighbor says: *we've lived here
close to 30 years. He will not share. Don't even ask.*

Nowadays, I need to slice a nice Northern Spy
into neat pieces before I take a bite.

>At the market, fruit after fruit after fruit.
>But only apples are the apple of my eye.

>The neighbor's sign reads, *please! I am the man
>who planted this old tree. All of its fruit belongs to me.*

Or maybe not. His house is catty-corner from my door. I keep
to my side of the street; can't read the sign from here.

And yet I peer across the way, see how the apples dangle
full-ripe and all aglow on autumn afternoons

or only spectral, lit by October's moon.

Reliquary

"Lose something every day. Accept the fluster . . . "
—Elizabeth Bishop

Every once in a while I open
one of too-many, tiny

boxes, and there you are,
bright stab of memory: My brave

lover from long ago. I see you
exactly as you were then, because

time took care to preserve the details,
the way amber traps an insect

for eternity. One could almost
map the genome from this fossil:

golden ring with its garnet chip.
I used to wear it on my little finger.

There are things we find
that were never hidden

even if we didn't know
exactly where they were.

Nothing of this kind is ever
lost, though after countless years

of practice, we may think
we have mastered that delicate art.

Before we all took names

Even days free of a blanket of crumpled lists
are rare. What span of modern time escapes at least
some dim assessment, even if merely toggled
back and forth between judgments? Good day. Bad week.

Our slow steps toward knowing more are not to blame.
Pre-history told us little, even doing its best. Midden. Potsherd.
Arrowhead. Cave wall. The ancestors were all individuals
perforce, but survivors of every catastrophe leaned toward

surviving the next. If there were names early on,
we no longer know them. How much of the saga
of our success was luck; how little was merit? It serves us
nothing to stare through the strata for an explanation—

there never was a year without a reckoning.
Volcano and tsunami year. Bad maize harvest year.
Heaviest winter in memory year. The year of the plague.
A single label may not capture the characteristics

of an entire era, but ours is the age of documentation.
Evidence everywhere. Disaster probably visible from Mars.

Four

Let the skull be a bowl

A question came to mind the other day when I doubled
mirrors so that I was there, and there, and there, as far back
as the eye could see. And I pictured this skull of mine without
the rest of me, surveyed my skull's cracked places, four deep
dents that remember blows from some unknown
enemy who felled me on the street half a lifetime ago.

In the absence of a better vessel, the top of the skull
would serve, once the brain is lost or taken. Go ahead.
Scrub it clean of its first material, let it bake
in medicinal sun, be rinsed in rain. Call it a bone
bowl, readily cupped in the palm and able to hold
a meal. What's to eat?

Sometimes it is necessary to cast the imagination
on a long line over the waters of history, so that the lure
sinks into a time about which little can truly be known.
Yes, there are artifacts. Maybe I didn't invent the idea
that this small basin could have been worked on, carefully,
by an ancestor, then kept to hold cooked tubers or grain.

And what if I hadn't survived? Could my skull have become
a receptacle? Would its flaws be visible during every meal?
Would the places where the bone was broken
and never got a chance to heal
make the bowl less of a prize to its new owner?
Or maybe more.

Still Scraping the Floor

(after Caillebotte)

Because sunlight from the window lands on the postcard where it hangs at work to hearten me when I am weary, the colors on the 4x6 inch image are now faded and untrue, though they were always tones of brown and beige, never bright colors. But my mental picture of the piece the way it looks on museum walls is faithful: the honest muscles on the worker to my right tell of his youth and years of labor; no sign yet of the softness that too much wine from that bottle on the table might add, decades down the road. He's talking to (or at least glancing sidelong at) the equally-fit fellow working next to him; off to the left of center is the third laborer, and my brow does furrow at the thought of how or why the workers occupy those separate spaces, different angles made by their relation to the half-scraped floor. For some who linger, breath held, before this piece in the museum, it is the muted hues, or the strange perspective of the floor that draws and holds the eye; others revel in the daring bareness of the backs and shoulders of these men—controversial exposure of the male physique at the Salon de Paris in 1875. For me, it is the light: a light I think must be unique to certain crooked streets in quiet quarters; this light that reaches in through floor-to-ceiling windows, catches the balcony of whimsical wrought iron; a light that to this day creeps close to admire what is beautiful.

Maybe I was eight years old. Maybe nine.

When the stars moved, I held onto the earth
with both arms splayed wide on the blanket beneath me.
I was alone in the back yard: a rarity.
I was alone and fearless in that moment. Also rare.

It was summertime. The air was damp and fragrant.
The stars stared at me. They did not blink, or twinkle.
I don't recall seeing the moon, nor noticing its absence.
Having the whole sky to myself astonished me.

How is it I never knew the planets moved, before then?
How could I think the constellations would stand still?
Flat on my back, I rode the earth, held on for dear life—
a wild ride, at a speed that made me dizzy, just a little.

There may have been something like music in the starscape
and the Milky Way was a smooth sheet drifting over me.

"Blumenfenster"

Without its abandoned friend, the astonishing view, my dining-table sits in front of the kitchen wall, where a painting I've studied all my life does its best to be cheerful. Tucked into the frame, its name, *Blumenfenster,* one of too many oils we used to own, all by a long-dead German painter no one's ever heard of, except his kin.

Now I sit before an object that lays claim to the word, *window,* and pretend three vases, filled to the brim with flowers, once inspired my half-blind great-uncle to reach for rose madder, Venetian red, yellow primrose instead of the green and thundercloud grey that made most of his other images a guarantee of sadness, deep and long.

The dreamery

Such an odd thing to see on Sleep-o-Vision. Wall-to-wall
nuance, bursting at the seams with classic symbols.
Wasn't there a great horned owl? Definitely a door giving way
into a glade, a path edged with primroses, various colors.

And then, to have the dream twice the same night, barely
altered after a brief awakening. Same owl? Maybe
a different door. But dreams are flimsy—too
delicate to survive the microscope. The light of day

dispels them the way fog on the Bay shifts
from thin to gone once the sun walks in.
Fruitless to wonder *why this? why that?* where
dreams are concerned. Science has tried for years

to hammer theories into submission. But that's just what happens
when you try to nail water onto water.

"House moving 'rained-out'"

(headline Dec. 1, 1982, Vincennes Sun-Commercial, Vincennes, Indiana)

I see they sold the old place, peeled off the front porch,
sawed it in two, top to bottom. Nailed strong plastic side to side

but the way the wind whips through this time of year
that won't keep the wet out long, and it takes a while

to tow two halves of a creaky clapboard building
from one state to another, plus you need the escorts

one ahead, one behind, with their flashing lights
to let the world know there's a house on its way.

And now this rain has washed out the move for today
as if this were a baseball game or a parade,

a rock concert or some other big deal.
Plus the forecast is for storms that give no refunds—

bluster and blow, torrents and possible floods
on the east-west road. How will we get these ceilings

transported, fixtures dangling, walls where you can see
holes for the pictures, closet with the rod all bowed,

wooden stairs with one squeaky board? Well,
Indiana to Oregon, or bust. Even if it is December.

The Auspices

See the tops of trees waving gently midway up the view?
        the view outside this window changes, hour by hour
hour after hour, we take for granted the bizarre mechanism
        that is a body—
  a body performing its cryptic tasks without interruption

Without interruption or any more instruction than was issued
        on Day One
  Day One: the heart is told to pump in fine weather or foul,
        sync with the lungs
(the lungs—when you went to the exhibit of the blacksmith's
        toil, they said . . .
  they said the bellows work like your lungs, but that seemed
        silly then)

Silly then; silly now: the lungs, the heart, and unsung organs
        even more
  even more easily taken for granted (think about your spleen?
        You don't)
you don't think of your benisons at all unless you're pushed
        to do so
  to do so, all you need is five blessed senses, or six, if
        you're lucky

You're lucky: every time you cease your agitation, it's obvious—
yes, obvious. Now watch the magpies dance. Tell me what you see

Nightmared

They're marred by all the dire, those hours when sweet sleep
is intended but impossible. Stacked in recollection, one
upon the shoulders of another, each scene resists interpretation.

Say I told these stories to a shrink, unfurled each episode
like a story-board, spoke them without undue inflection.
What do you make of these, O oracle?

> Well, the cimbal is an obvious symbol, just as the totem
> pole was clearly an omen; the flying and the falling
> are almost too easy—same as the test
> in trigonometry, or the sudden nudity.

I rarely dream of dragons, and my important dead
make cameo appearances, if any, even though they occupy
day-mind like valiant soldiers, never asking to be relieved.

Blind brain in each night's pillowed head, why do you scour
each landscape for the fearsome? Am I not equipped with adequate
mystery, walking the world by day with my eyes open?

Dwindle

The word sounds sweet to your ear, doesn't it?
Even endearing, as though the accent
is on the diminutive. Use the word
when the blizzard *dwindles:* people are grateful.

Not so when what dwindles is hope. It's hard
to wave farewell to health, or a steady
income, or the prospect of fine times
with one's beloved, cheek by jowl, on a jaunty

walk through a world not yet marred by
the inevitable. Oh. Now you remind me: this planet
screams, spits, burns with indignation at all our
affronts. How soon will we be shown the permanent

consequences of our heedlessness? Say goodbye
to the darling and the green. Because the inevitable
does not dwindle. Its bags are always packed
with necessity. What's unavoidable

marches through our ranks wearing a pall,
ready for anything except an alternative.

Spectrum

in the before-light of the winter
solstice, all things are held
in one breath: the sky spilling
its darkness into the adjacent
latitude; colors almost too pale to name
seep back first.

now morning breaks earlier here
and later there, in the antipodes.
my faraway sister's weather, still
strange in its annual unfamiliarity.
summer nights breathless for me
while, clad in wool, she stokes the fire.

Two messengers speak, in passing

fragrance of another time
creates mischief in my mind

it can happen in August—
even here with our salt-wind
Mediterranean air—sharp gust

plucks a fistful of leaves
and rattles them down

the pavement to scatter summer
out of the path,
introduce the sharp

scent of a different season/
latitude/geography

when I was someone else and
could not possibly imagine my
current self

        how is this done? This strange
        magic whereby aromas

        assemble on the signal from
        some displaced component

        and the mixture, admitted
        through a single sense,
        overwhelms the others

        to re-constitute a place, an
        instant in my story,
        whisper-dim

        until this moment   merciful
        brevity of such time-travel

        I nearly wrote "travail"
        because the gods know just
        how hard it is

    being absolutely present for one minute
just once   or maybe twice, when memory allows

Countdown

        Already, the absence of an image
        draws attention to the space
        where Wrights Lake (yes,
        Wrights Lake, not *Wright's* Lake)
        perched on the bedroom wall.
        Ghostly in memory, lines of the
        rocks, water, rowboat, pines
        around the lake no longer stark,
        deep-carved into a linoleum
        block that yielded this numbered
        print by an artist friend.

No shadow betrays the picture's old position,
but my eyes perform the necessary pentimento.

    Bit by bit, this familiar address yields
    its claim to the name *home.* An empty bookshelf
    looms in the living room. I've packed the contents
    of the only antique item, remembered
    its position in sundry prior houses, even heard (almost)
    my long-dead mother's voice reminding me
    sewing scissors are in the walnut cupboard,
    left-hand drawer.

These days, moving is not only no picnic,
    it's the terrain of a kind of fathomless contemplation.
        Half the stuff I touch asks *do you really need this?*
All of it challenges me to visualize one final
    move, in which I can take nothing,
        absolutely nothing with me.

Incarnation

We all look out of the same eyes, if we have eyes,
but the heart keeps track of what we see. And yet, heart
is to fist as muscle is to trouble; trickster mind
an everyday cornucopia. Once, before our innocence

freckled, perception was self-regulated. We
had to learn to apply admonitions in a strictly
binary way. *Go* and *Stay* were not yet opposites, because
verbs behaved more like everyday carp in a koi pond.

What happened? These days, a kneejerk propels us
toward longing when we turn our gaze outward.
Inter-species wistfulness? Some of us peer at hypothetical
x-rays and see baleen when we search for ambergris.

Or vice versa. Then everything flashes an irredeemable
green. Because this is the bardo. Not a weird dream.

"Skin hunger"

That my flesh is relentlessly thirsty has been true
for years: with the juice my youth used to generate
long gone, the Mojave now papers my arm.

But I just learned a term that frightens me—
one of those phrases that, once read, reverberates
inside your head like a temple gong.

This morning's find derailed me. Who knows
if I will suffer from this strange disorder—
me, solo for all these years, plus months

plus days. It was details from the experiment
that rocked my soul: the obscure scientist who found
that baby monkeys would choose starvation to stay

with a pseudo-mother made of softest wool over survival
spent with a creature made of metal that would feed it milk,
but couldn't cuddle worth a damn.

Moratorium

What are we waiting for? A woman? Two trees?
—André Breton

Waiting for two trees to become ten trees;
to become a forest. Or waiting for two trees
to become one tree, obliged to press together
bark and bark, until their edges merge
with barely a scar.

Waiting for the tree beneath which little girls
in summer dresses lay prone as we piped our careless
song—will not that tree return in our great age,
sheltering the same halcyon day
beneath its branches?

Waiting for the ancient tree that has been leaning,
gently leaning, its shallow roots defiant
for one thousand years, disobedient of the usual
rules, to be brought finally, suddenly
into compliance with immutable law

and thus to fall, heard or unheard, and close
the door to its life as a vertical being;
begin its long death, its metamorphosis
to an infinity of dust, when Sempervirens
has offered all it had in the service of its habitat

and now has nothing more to do.

Lately, certain months decline their customary duty

Like this April, limping into May. You see me
fallow, as though fixed rigid in the opposite season—
leaves in decay, every blossom withered, chill descending
deeper and deeper into the stiff ground. You see me

un-inked. You see me empty-handed, fingers slack
even though tools strew the table. Normally, April's spring-fed
rivulets pull richness forth. In bygone years abundance
veered toward embarrassing even the most greedy

of April's ritual participants. What happened here?
Fond of a mystery as I normally am, I worry this one harbors
horror in its sharp corners. I will be forensic: I will glean
via observation what traps were sprung. Time will not

muddle my investigation, brief as the window's opening
may be. I must know more. Fear less. Tug every tiny tendril.

Consider two comrades, quiet and silence

What we call silence here, closed in for two short
days, does not mean there is no sound.
Remove the chatter from a group of people
even for just a couple of hours, you'll still

hear footsteps on the wooden floors, other
footsteps on a gravel path outdoors, the rattle
of ill-fitting sash windows as the wind stirs.
Machines are hard at work somewhere, keeping

water hot; they're audible in some subsonic way.
Someone shifts a plastic box a few inches.
The air from out of doors will carry
car noise, though not as much as in the city.

Even if the kitchen is at a distance,
something will clang or bang as cooks
create the mid-day meal. And making art
won't happen in a vacuum: little

clicks as brushes swirl in cups of water
when you shift from one color to another—
some tiny vibration trickles through the room.
This pen. This page. Someone's sigh.

"Everything we see hides another thing"

These words were hidden under Notes
on my device. I thought I had written them
myself and admired how clever I must be.

Then I noticed the quotation marks, so
I went to the oracle and asked: *who wrote
these words that are both ordinary and true?*

When the answer came: *it was of course
the artist, Magritte* I was aghast. Not that
I begrudged him the credit by any means

but because the knowledge bolstered a concern
I've had for years about the human mind: how hard
it has to work to make a memory and then file it

safe and sound so that it comes next time you call.
I had an aunt who told me more than once
she feared her mental faculties would fail

before her antique body took her down. And then
they did, leaving her stranded, abandoned
by the capacity that builds a story

block by block, bolts its components
invisibly to beams that will not shift.
Everything I see hides another thing,

and so I write, hopeful that words will steer me
through the labyrinth I entered
unseeable years, uncountable miles ago.

Carried, or buoyed

While I stood silent, smug-happy, the horseshoe
tipped, spilling all of my good fortune on the ground.
Seep! And then the earth grew cheerful; the wide sky
drew up each bead of moisture that remained

and made clouds, ten kinds of clouds. Beneath them,
branches of trees seemed to hear the call to waltz, though
there was no music. Under the silence, a whisper
as if bliss were stirring.

Oh! so to share my good luck was a boon? To lose
myself into the earth meant new pools of contentment.
Sweet-water springs arose when my senses acknowledged
the dazzle. Have I not always known I am only

a vessel? I carry what chooses me, and everything in me
will be transmuted and restored, cell by cell.

About the Author

Annie Stenzel is a lesbian who was born in Illinois, but did not stay put. Her first full-length collection is *The First Home Air After Absence* (Big Table Publishing, 2017). A free-range poet who writes in and out of forms, her poems appear or are forthcoming in a wide array of print and online journals in the U.S. and the U.K., including *Atlas and Alice, Chestnut Review, Galway Review, Kestrel, Night Heron Barks, One Art, Pine Hills Review, Rust & Moth, Saranac Review, SoFloPoJo, SWWIM, The Lake,* and *UCity Review*. Her work has been nominated several times for the Pushcart Prize and Best of the Net. She is also a poetry editor/reader for the online journals *Right Hand Pointing* and *West Trestle Review*. She currently lives on unceded Ohlone land within walking distance of the San Francisco Bay, and pays a voluntary monthly land tax to help restore Indigenous life.

www.ingramcontent.com/pod-product-compliance
Lightning Source LLC
Chambersburg PA
CBHW030911170426
43193CB00009BA/806